# THE GIRL WHO CRIED

# THE GIRL WHO CRIED

*Charlotte Gann*

HAPPENSTANCE

BY THE SAME AUTHOR:

*Noir*, HappenStance, 2016
*The Long Woman*, Pighog, 2011

ACKNOWLEDGEMENTS:

Thanks are due to editors of the following, in which versions of some of these poems first appeared: *The Compass*, *Finished Creatures*, *Iota* , *The Long Woman* (Pighog), *Morphrog*, *The North*, *Poetry & All That Jazz*, *The Rialto*, *Snakeskin* and *Truths* (Telltale Press). Two of the line drawings were included in *Viva Lewes*. A version of 'The idea is' (page 30) was in *Noir*, HappenStance 2016.

NOTE FOR VISUALLY IMPAIRED READERS:

The book jacket is reddish umber, with panels of mustard yellow on both front and back jackets. The front has a broad band of yellow starting just above the middle and occupying in total about one third of the jacket. All text is centred on this panel, first the author's name in dark red italics, then a small red leaf ornament, then the title in caps. The back jacket has descriptive text in white lower case at the top, followed by a reviewer endorsement centred in yellow. Below this, a mustard yellow box holds a sample poem ('We do not want to know about the rocks', p. 10) in dark red type. Bottom left is a drawing of a head bobbing above water with two black eyes, like a seal. Many poems inside have illustrations in a similar style.

First published in 2020 by HappenStance Press
21 Hatton Green, Glenrothes KY7 4SD
www.happenstancepress.com

ISBN: 978-1-910131-61-9



Printed and bound by Imprint Digital, Exeter
https://digital.imprint.co.uk

*Whatever wind blows, while they and I have leaves*
*We cannot other than an aspen be*
*That ceaselessly, unreasonably grieves,*
*Or so men think who like a different tree.*

—Edward Thomas, from 'Aspens'

# THE GIRL WHO CRIED

*'There are things,' she says, 'which are difficult,
perhaps impossible to talk about.'*

*for Alex*
*& other allies*

❐

Nobody wants to know about me, or this.
Nobody. You want 'an easy life'.
Nothing to do with me. Or nothing
complicated. Me, I want to be loved.
You want to be left alone.
I want that too. Just not by you.

❐

We do not want to know about the rocks.
Of course, occasionally someone disappears
but it's better, safer, to keep things

as they are. Imagine what would happen
if we lit up this stretch of water? The dark
would come alive with shapes and creatures.

The rocks would rear up jagged. We'd see
how deep the water really is: those
lonely fathoms. Besides, just think,

what might we glimpse below the surface?
Lost faces—*imagine*? The fright! Don't fret.
People drown silently most of the time.

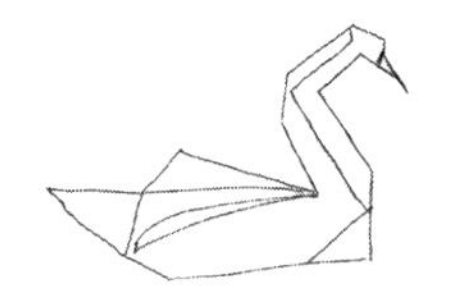

❒

You asked if I wanted a walk.

I nodded, in silence. Then started
to talk. Every time you looked away

I grabbed your sleeve. I slipped pebbles
in your pockets: weighed you down.

You were very patient. We walked for miles.

❐

The problem is that I bring need into the equation.
It doesn't belong here. It's not welcome.

*We're sorry for any inconvenience caused.*

The problem is that need looks a lot like neediness.
And who wants that? Especially from an odd direction.

*We're sorry for any inconvenience caused.*

Need is a bottomless pit. It's never fruitful.
It's a burden and a pittance and a pointless spectacle.

*We're sorry for any inconvenience caused.*

IT'S NOT WANTED HERE.
Hide your need away, or make yourself scarce.

*We're sorry for any inconvenience caused.*

Come on, tuck yourself in, take yourself out, pop that
need away on the highest, furthest shelf.

*We're sorry for any inconvenience caused.*

You can do it: you've been doing it your whole life.
Put your need in a box and bury it in your chest.

*We're sorry for any inconvenience caused.*

Smile. Go about your business and pretend to be okay.
Life will be over before you know it. Life will be over.

*We're sorry for any inconvenience.*

❒

The urgency of anger passes. Outside,
chalk cliffs soften with grass and bracken.
We're nervous of the teenagers who clamber

the banks at night to smoke and drink
under the moon, safe from adult eyes.
Only yesterday they were us, tomorrow

it'll be our kids. The long white road
is tarmacked over now. In the print,
there's chalk dust coating everything,

a fine white film. I can't just reach inside
the house, tip it. Pluck up the figure
who stands in dark unbreachable silence.

That woman who long ago pushed up
the window, lowered the blind
and disappeared backwards

out of the window frame, withdrew
(like me) from flat low sky—clammy
fingers, prying eyes—into her cool interior.

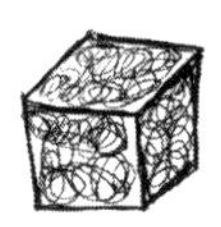

❐

I drew tiny devils round the house.
I drew them round my hours.
I drew them in pencil on the walls
so small no one noticed they
were there at all.
I drew them on the skirting boards.
I swept the yard
and filled the coal scuttle
in the frightening dark.
And I crept down the garden
far beyond the light that spilled
from the sitting room window
and I shut the bantams in at night
so they weren't dismembered.
And I polished my father's shoes
kneeling on newspaper on Sundays.
And I laboured alongside Void
who always looked dishevelled

while Null—
whom I loved with all my heart—
had everything.

❐

I knew my teacher drove that way—
twice a day—in her golden Saab.
So I took the steps three at a time,

all of a sudden, the rusted handrail
grazing my palm. I never knew
if I was running away—or towards

the small black block of light at the top
where the streetlight shed its beam
across the wet spattered gloom

and the flight opened onto
the narrow pavement and the stream
of cars shot past in the dark.

❐

I breathe in clouds of chalk dust
left in her empty classroom.
Place my hand inside
an off-pink handprint on a desk.
Relive an absent kiss
on the farthest reaches of my hair.

I find a stub of chalk.
'She's coming back,' it says.

❐

Flame-faced, furious, pissed again
I'm slumped on a wooden stool
in a boyfriend's mum's magic kitchen.

It's gone midnight. The street light's
bleaching her rubber gloves, chrome sink,
draining board. I give myself

fifteen minutes' grace to wait, in flames,
on the off chance she'll wander in
from the next room where she's sitting,

talking quietly with her child-psychologist
husband, watching TV in the blue light,
her knitting needles clicking.

❐

My tin comforts me. Battered, dented,
it jangles against my pencil case.

In lessons, I reach for it in the dark of my satchel
and coil it snugly into one hand.

I crack it open later, up on the Downs alone.
One whiff of moist tobacco, a chestnut curl,

clouded sheaths of paper. *Tap, tap.*
That rush of petrol. The iron spark at its centre

shooting along, under cover, between my lips
down my throat, into my lungs—

sacks of folded blackness. How I need to feel
fire burn into cold unopened spaces.

❐

Work days float morning unaligned to afternoon night another country

I'm laying out type while thoughts jam and spool overmatter

Links break hopes sink (deadweights) or gape

I waste all my high resolution on never saving

It's time to settle on a suitcase with which to face things

except love which runs behind everything never around

❐

Clients queue for your time, line your hall
like coats, wait for their allotted hour.

There is a girl coming through
much thicker and darker than me.

She doesn't keep things neatly in boxes.
She pirouettes in torn tights,

leaves blood on your sofa,
never sticks to appointment times.

Poor loves, because they're hungry
they think they've fed—

no matter how many lamps you light
your room will never recover—

their faces, so big and earnest,
spinning like plates behind their umbrellas.

Woe betide the kind of woman who might
loom in your frosted glass,

a woman who *can* meet your eyes,
*tell* you she's hungry.

❐

I leave the pub alone,
zig-zag back

to the stench of Mrs Docker's
boiled cabbage in the hall,

to the stab of latch key,
to the rising tide

of dirty clothes and coffee cups,
to my arc leap

from door to bed
to sleep adrift

with a rescue cat so lonely
she purrs all night

in the seaweed hammock
of my hair.

❐

Whenever I cry for help, he comes,
rings the doorbell he put in.
I answer in a man's shirt.

He's wearing sky-blue overalls.
I watch him climb to see inside
my broken curtain rail.

Our faceless children
boomerang along
corridors I've never seen.

When he leaves, I collapse,
now stripped and melting.
He wouldn't know me.

He is enormous in my dreams,
my flat key curling in his palm
like one of those red fishes.

❐

He drops me at the highest point
where tufted grass meets tarmac.

White with shock I press
my head to his, two stripped fox skulls

on his dashboard. Then I'm gone.
Sliding off hard leather.

I sense him crane to wave
but I am flung

out of the frame, falling away
along the side of his white van.

❒

For years there is this walking woman,
walking, walking, hooded, boots white with chalk.
Along the sides of busy A-roads,
drivers clock her: one beat, one black blink.
'We would never taunt her.' And then one day
she's gone.
Back in that room with thin curtains,
a baby bulges, forces passage;
taps her milk with short sharp beak; grows stick legs,
a jagged mop of hair, wide shiny eyes;
is off to school.
And back and forth she walks
and walks, hooded, upright. And every day
she crosses at the same place, drops down
a twitten. Seagulls scream and twist, metal
sea rises.
On she walks: her child needs her.

❐

the spider's web

is suspended from twigs in the light
& at night

it can be snapped        repaired

or   utterly broken
swept up off   out of our hair & faces

or   it can hang here invisibly
where nobody notices

❐

At the end of my climb
I stumble on an amber pond,
all milky greens and gold.

The view beyond is washed in pale blue,
as if a child had toppled
his jar of water.

Suddenly something darker stirs,
just creasing the surface,
exciting the birds.

I sense some threat,
take in a knot of angry
hawthorns muttering.

And then I see one
standing alone,
all fingers and space,

holding its frozen pose,
facing one way,
the way the wind has made it.

And I see me. Bleak, brittle,
almost ridiculous,
and mauve with loneliness.

❐

We coincided on a road island.

I spotted her familiar figure creeping
round the edge of the war memorial.

She looked tiny, brittle, strangely luminous
as she hobbled on a stick towards me.

She smiled, greeted, continued crossing.

❐

Here's how it starts.
I look up a word you've said to me.
Search for hidden depth
and meaning.
Take that one thread and try
to spin a yarn from it.
Grab that, work outwards.
Pull, pull on the thread,
trying to fashion
a covering,
to discover some secret
sewn into its lining....

Yesterday I read
'I loved you
as much as you
wanted me to;
it made no difference.'
And only today you wrote
'I can send love.
It is not enough.
It will never be
enough. But
it is something.'

❐

‘Not that you’re obsessed or anything’, she said,
leaning towards me, smirking. *Christ.* She pulled
on her fag, blew out the smoke with a little snort.

It’s at its worst in the evenings. As night-time
approaches, my fingers linger, tingling, my face
bent taut towards the blue light of my screen.

‘Sorry,’ I said. ‘I was just trying to grill bacon
while checking my email….’ How the hell
could this have happened? How could I

have ended up calling *her* this god-forsaken
Sunday morning? This bloody life. How to pick up
the pieces *again.* How to find the strength.

❒

The idea is
you stand here, shuffle along and
when your turn comes she'll
sign your book, and hug you.
Under these arches, though, even
the pigeons are freezing;
the girls ahead and behind me
are both turned, facing others.
The tide's coming in and it's
soaked my plimsolls.
The queue stretches as far as I can
see in both directions.
I'm scared, of course, of losing
my place but the woman
in the distance, signing books
is enunciating
each person's name
carefully, once,
through a tannoy.
I yearn to be closer
but the queue never gets shorter
and the woman stays
small as a worry doll
on the horizon.

❐

| | |
|---|---|
| *Are we close* | YES, we're close |
| *Are we close* | Yes, we're close :) |
| *Are we close* | YES, I really like you |
| *Are we close* | Yes, don't worry |
| *Are we close* | Um— |
| | |
| *Are we close* | Please don't keep asking |
| *Are we close* | Just. Be. In. It. |
| *Are we close* | Not as close as family |
| *Are we close* | Not like lovers! |
| *Are we close* | Not like *old* friends |
| | |
| *Are we close* | YES, we're close. |
| *Are we close* | I think I said... |
| *Are we close* | — |
| *Are we close* | Not *that* close |
| *Are we close* | |

❐

'You live in a strange world all your own making.'

'How do you square The Woman who
is perfect, so important to you,
with The Woman who couldn't care less?'

'Exclusion is what you can't bear
but when you do get inside
you find it's not safe.'

○

Today T.W. is wearing trousers for the first time.

I'm busy punching out cake shapes in pastry:
when I *can* come here; when I can't.

Beyond that, there are now no defined edges.

○

Each day, pinned to her headboard are scraps of
notes from A. N. Other. She puts them there to show me
that the rest of her life is real. The pair
of them are clearly close and growing closer.

○

My raft is made of blocks of speech.
Why won't she help me? Her life may be
serene but mine is bitty: perched
on the edge of my bed, palms sweating.

○

So I am in India drinking tea with T.W.
and there are these creatures, half horse, half elephant,
perched high on a ledge like birds. Every now and then
one jumps, taking the width of the street to land.

We sit at our table and watch. They leap,
one after another, a great spectacle, until suddenly
I notice the last one has stumps—raw, bloody stumps—
for front legs. It could not, would *never*
be able to jump.

○

If only we could go somewhere nice, a nice tea,
just the two of us. A small sweet cottage.
White teapot. Everything white. And go to sleep.

'We are unbearably close, or very very distant.'

This is what she keeps on telling me.

❐

Lighting a furnace inside an envelope
is not something you'd suggest a child do.

Not something you could honestly say
had 'worked', for you. Not something

you'd recommend exactly—or post
to Facebook with a smiley emoji. No.

❐

I let go. The waves are cold.
I flap, spin round—you
haven't gone far, you might
yet turn (I know you won't).

A sob takes hold.
I'm treading water, trying
to think ('Don't *think*;
float,' you said). *Can* I float?

❒

Each time you leave
it kicks me so hard
my breath can't

come back until
you come back.

Guilt, shame.
Shame, guilt.
I'm not allowed

to feel
the things I feel.

❐

Sometimes I've sat opposite you
and built an idea of who you are—
your soft edges—

and then your phone has rung and you've
answered it, or pulled a magazine
or tabloid from your bag

or glanced across at me
and looked right through me
and there's been no warmth at all.

❐

When I heard your voice on the line,
and you said 'Look, at least let me tell you
how it seemed to me,' frankly I felt relieved—

here was someone else alive inside these
looping telephone wires. And yes, I was
scared (& hurt & angry & sad) and you

were clearly exasperated, and yet
none of this seemed to spell disaster.
Instead, I could sense the intricacies

of another human being—breathing,
(smiling?), waiting, then articulating.
Our whole argument left me calmer.

❐

She filled a bath and locked the door.
She kept the taps running till the bath overflowed.
The black water seeped under the green door,
growing in a silent pool. A cat burst
in. Sniffed, snorted, flattened its ears.
No other sound, just running water.

And then ... something else. An animal groan.
We got our mops. Started trying to get the place back
in order. The floor was lethal,
the cat was feral. And the restaurant was calling.
It seemed easier to leave the flat. But surely
we had to get her at least to turn off
the water? Leave the mess. But *stop the water.*

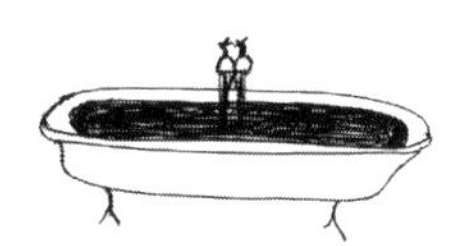

❒

*Jesus Christ Almighty,* I've been lugging this thing around a long time now. All my life, I reckon. It's actually heavier than it looks: *very* awkward to carry. And I can't *ever* put it down. Not for one *second.* It gets in the way of tasks is putting it mildly. Some years I've tried to fit a person's face to it: as though that might at least make my carrying it seem worthwhile, or like it has some point, or *purpose.* I have wondered too whether this might make me less *lonely*. Plus, once I've got a person's face in mind, I can't forget it, or not for an intense old time at least: it's like their face is *perfect*.... Of course, this never works either. Why *would* some poor passing stranger want to make that kind of pledge to me? Have their image, life-sized, hauled around by *me*? No one's ever given the go-ahead is the long and short of it. And the damn frame remains empty, with jagged nails sticking out to catch on things—and on me—and drive me crazy.

❒

The house with no door looks welcoming,
with its wisteria and robins. I can see,

through the kitchen window, a bowl
of cherries. They're the brightest, darkest,

shiniest cherries. But that window's shut
and bolted. I move on round. I know

I shouldn't walk on flowerbeds.
I keep thinking the door must be around

the next corner. I've lost count now
how many times I've circumnavigated.

❒

Being on the phone with you

is like skating on ice—
or rather, watching an ice skater.

I am spectator, as this figure
shoots round and round a frozen floor

past me, past me,
again and again.

❒

My brother's skin itches, like a coat
he can't scrape off.

His heart pumps doggedly.
Yanking his shirt on—

over all this—is difficult.
One sleeve catches

and he yearns to rip his
nuisance doll's arm off.

End the misery in blood.
He tackles his buttons—

*fucking* fiddly things, plus
two at the veins on

his wrists. He stares in
the mirror. Back at him,

hard-eyed, comes that look.
His glasses glisten. He

needs to be *held.*
The bathroom floor is spinning.

His bag stands in the hall.
Where is the fucking taxi?

❐

It's 6 a.m. and I'm camping on her doorstep.
You see, the night was filled with much-too-
big things. I want to tell her about them.
I want her to hear, and I want to hear
what she says back. I know it will be kind or funny.
It will make the day better, the night....

That flat white sky outside is as blank
and bleak as these weeks of waiting—
these years—and our children
grow older, taller, draw their own lives
round them like half-stitched coats.
I'm not finished, though I feel it—exhausted

from the thing that grows up still inside me.
How can I wake at fifty
with the same pain I woke with aged five?
But I do, I *do*. It wakes me even though I tell it
I'm exhausted, this can surely wait
till morning. It doesn't and it can't.

❒

Thirst is all too real
when you can't turn your own taps.
When you have to rely on visitors
to twist them for you.

The risk of flooding
is also great when you need to wait
for their next visit
to turn those damn taps off again.

❒

It's dead quiet. I'm staring at the wall. A certain peace
in silence. Stay still, don't make a sound, barely breathe—

listen. I look out at the yellow tree. I'm tired
but it's light now in the yellow branches.

I live on a ledge. At some point my ex brings food
and I have to hide. I'm dragging my bursting cat basket

through a crowded station. My anxious brother
hurries us, clutching a newspaper and sandwiches.

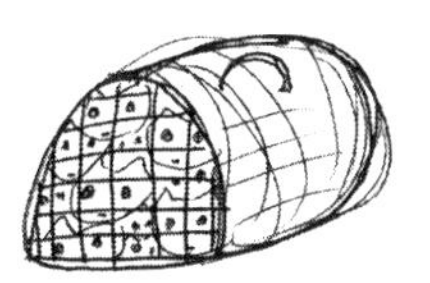

❐

^tt^chment

we find a thing to be obsessed with
l^tch ourselves on and drill down

into it (this ^tt^ches us firmly
to the rock) we build a sm^ll

roof ^bove us really just
^ hat (it looks like this

^) so we're BUSY now
^nd h^ve a SHELTER

S^FE (until we're
not) h^rd h^tted

until we're
^nyw^y

crush-
ed

❐

My 'remnant' she called it.

When I made my admission (no names,
dates, just the severity of the condition)
we both almost laughed! Surely
I'd grown out of this by now?
Do we carry the babies we were
inside us our whole lives?

We were walking on top of the world,
along a scraggly, black, gritty path,
August heat in April. It wasn't bliss.
It was real: two friends staggering,
attempting to compare notes. I said
'So *I* must fear I'm unlovable'—

and realise now the same thing
erupted two years earlier. Then
I was out walking with an older pal
(and she, by the by, a professional).
We sat together on scorched grass
beside a broken, rusting plough.

I cried and cried, and it was then
she coined the term.

❒

Hands pressed to jumper; arms wrapped around her.
  In the film, towards the end, often there is
      this reconciliation.

Two rush forward, meet in a long, known embrace.
  Given, and received. As we watch, fingers clutch
at wool, then relax. Hold their pose.

A press of self to self, body to body.
  Often a hand holds a head to a shoulder.
Two humans fit together.

❒

Around eleven every Saturday morning
I press my finger to your doorbell. Glance
at my phone or across the street—usually

someone I recognise—turn back to your
door: the mottled window with its iron
veins. Press my head closer, peer. The air

is whiter in places: if I tilt my head,
it tilts. I wonder if you heard the bell?
If I telephone, you'll probably answer.

This is always the moment when the light
shifts slowly; slowly rearranges itself
into the small mass of your moving person.

❒

'Your frame is f***ed; that's your problem. On the plus side, knock it two inches to the right, and that'll solve everything.' This is what I finally saw at 5 a.m. this morning. I'm usually awake, these days, gaping in through that hour-window; this thought, however, was new. And welcome. In through the door, processed, immediately, in technicolor, husband, and sons. Also, I noted with relief, the hurt girl wasn't any longer left outside. She'd taken a break from hurling sharp objects, or meticulously mapping suicide, and was slumped in that red wooden chair we used to have in the kitchen. Someone had put a blanket around her and she was crying but inside the frame.

❒

She was ironing, as she always did on Sundays,
and as I passed, paused—which wasn't usual—
the iron resting on a pale green shirt.

'Your life won't always be like this,' she said.
'This chapter now—when people close to you
keep dying—it will end. And then,' she said

'decades may pass, when no one very near
you dies. These are,' she said, 'your early
losses.' And then she carried on ironing.

❐

That's the table where two friends sat. Always
that one, by the painted radiator.
It was warm in winter, scalding. Still,
we always chose that table—set apart,
so people weren't too bothered by our chat.

Today I won't be lighting up. But
I see the outline of us where we sat—
heads together. We were talking then.
The barmaid's kind. When I leave we wave
like old pals. No need to call out thanks.

❐

When I came in this morning, the window
was full of birds. One hundred and three
of them chip chip chirruping.

❒

The water's silent: heavy, black and silent.
She's at its edge, on a steep mud bank.
She casts the thing. Carried by the weight
it drops into the plump of water,
disappears. The water ruffles closed;
nothing. No sign that she's been here.
The line glistens like spider-web.

❐

The ambulance had landed, like a UFO,
before I arrived (after the phone call).
It was sealed, so I paced round and round,

searching for a way in without knocking.
I'm your next of kin. They scooped me in.
How can such a situation feel like gain?

We're hurtling towards the hospital, towards
your death. You're vomiting blood into
the plastic mask that covers your face.
You're stripped to the waist.

We're held together even as we hurtle.
Held tight inside a silver box inside
a box: inside a capsule. Friday night
sirens muffled.
I'm with you.
*I'm with you.*

❒

I, who never iron, have dragged the board from under the bed
and creaked it open. I'm running the iron back and forth
across a white cotton nightie, wanting it perfect.

She sleeps, oblivious. When the trolley arrives, she stirs, opens
one eye, and hauls herself upright. She stabs blocks of beef,
coins of carrot, lifts the fork again and again to her mouth.

When I arrive, she peers at me once, sideways; then ignores me.
I sit beside her, quiet. When it's time, I say 'I'm going now.'
On the path, I look back. She's craning at a window. Waving.

❒

unframed
photographs

droop like tulips
their flimsy faces

black and white
catch the light
and glare

in time they slump
collapse

slide down
the book
spines

held only
by dust
they fall

come to rest
somewhere
behind things

when no one's
in the room

❐

They thought they knew me. What did they know?
The smile I wore—my kind of clothes.
They saw me out walking and they thought

*She likes walking*. They thought they knew
from the jokes I made (often muttered—
they'd smile awkwardly, not really hearing).

They thought I was okay. Last time
anyone wrote, I answered cheerfully.
Last time anyone wrote, I answered.

❒

When the waiter draws near,
my brother's eyes start their restless
flit back and forth, as do his fingers,
registering knife, fork, glass—mainly glass.
The waiter draws close, retreats again.
My brother looks momentarily, wildly,
happy. Continues with his speech—
how he's afraid and sorry, but can't
any longer offer cast-iron guarantees.

I reach across, touch his sleeve. He jerks
free of the table, free of me.
One small tear snakes across his face,
joins a rivulet of sweat. My brother
yanks off steamed-up glasses, pummels
them between folds of napkin.
He turns his sharp grey eyes on me.
'It's just I thought you should know,'
he says, now calm.

❐

'I couldn't care less!' the little boy yelled.
He was meant to be in school but wasn't.
He was here on the hill road. Four years old
and marching away from all of it

shouting, top of his voice, 'I'm out of here!'
Without a backward glance he stormed on down.
One teacher got on her phone. Another—
who'd seen it all before—thought she knew how

to follow him with a pro's detachment.
'Miles, I'm here to keep you safe,' she called.
'Fuck off,' he said. Then—but too quietly—
'It's not what I meant.' They were both appalled.

The road and his impossible life in
all its complexity stretched before him.

❐

Love. The word I said
into the telephone.

I had to say it three times
before it came out right.

'What,' you asked, 'what?'
Your voice was gentle.

The word fell and fell.
Did you catch it?

## ABOUT THE AUTHOR

Charlotte Gann grew up in Sussex, studied English at UCL and then worked in London. Her first job was proofreader for a typesetters in Clerkenwell; later she was editor of *Health Which?* in Marylebone. In her mid-30s she went freelance and moved to Brighton to start a family. She also began to write poetry, and did an MA in Creative Writing and Personal Development at the University of Sussex. In 2011, her debut pamphlet, *The Long Woman*, was published by Pighog Press and subsequently shortlisted for the Michael Marks Award. Her first full collection, *Noir*, came out from Happen*Stance* in 2016. She is editor of *Viva Lewes*, and also co-edits (and writes) OPOI reviews for sphinxreview.co.uk.